RUN EDIN-BURGH

great running routes in and around the city

The author and publisher have made every effort to ensure that the information in this publication is accurate, and accept no responsibility whatsoever for any loss, injury or inconvenience experienced by any person or persons whilst using this book.

published by
pocket mountains ltd
Holm Street, Moffat
Dumfries and Galloway
DG10 9EB

ISBN: 978-1-907025-23-5

Printed in Poland REP2015

Introduction

This book is for all types of runners – whether you are just starting out, a regular runner or training for a race.

Over five sections you will find interesting and varied runs of different distances – and on a mix of terrain – in and around Edinburgh.

The times given for each run are based on an average speed of 10 minutes per mile (timings are more generous for the hill runs in the Pentlands), but don't worry if you are faster or slower than this; it is simply intended as a rough guide to help you plan your run.

If you are new to running you're likely to have a lot of questions – the following pages should answer most of them ...

Why should I run?

If you need convincing, read the list below and you will have your trainers on in no time!

- Aids weight loss (on average for every mile you run you will burn around 100 calories – depending on your speed and weight)
- Elevates the levels of endorphins – 'the feel-good' hormone – even more than other cardiovascular exercise like swimming or cycling
- Decreases your blood pressure
- Improves the health of your lungs
- Lowers your cholesterol
- Stimulates blood circulation to improve the health of your skin
- Can help prevent osteoporosis
- Improves your quality of sleep
- Boosts your self-esteem and confidence
- Reduces your risk of developing heart disease, stroke, diabetes, colon cancer, breast cancer, anxiety and depression.

This guide aims to make it as easy as possible to get these benefits by sharing some of the most inspiring runs in and around the city.

What trainers do I need?

It is vital that you buy a good pair of running shoes to protect your joints. Always go to a good running shop to get advice. Edinburgh has several excellent retailers staffed by experienced runners who provide a fitting service.

Tips for buying trainers

- Wear athletic socks when trying shoes on
- Running shoes don't need to be broken in: if they pinch don't buy
- Shop later in the day when your feet are bigger
- Better to have two pairs; both will last longer, especially if you clean and dry them between runs
- Don't play other sports in them, especially football!
- Do your laces up criss-cross: a good running shop will show you how
- After cleaning, stuff them with newspaper and leave in an airy place: never dry them on a radiator
- Know when to bin them: regardless of price the cushioning will go after 300-400 miles. There is a risk of injury if you persist in running in worn-out shoes.

What should I wear?

If you are going to get serious about your running, you should think about buying clothes designed for the job. Buy fabrics that wick: that is, they are designed to move moisture away from your body, allowing it to evaporate quickly. Don't wear cotton: it absorbs sweat making you feel heavy and uncomfortable, which in turn makes you sweat more, causing dehydration and fatigue.

Edinburgh running shops

Sweatshop

David Lloyd Leisure, Newhaven Harbour, Leith EH6 4LX
www.sweatshop.co.uk

Run-4-It

108-110 Lothian Road, EH3 9BE
www.run4it.com

Run and Become

20 Queensferry Street, EH2 4QW
www.runandbecome.com

Footworks

14-17 Bruntsfield Place, EH10 4HN
www.footworks-uk.com

The Tri Centre

57-59 South Clerk Street, EH8 9PP
www.thetricentre.com

Food and drink

Ideally you should eat a small snack 1-2 hours before you run, and then within 30-60 minutes of finishing in order to replace energy and give your body the bricks needed to repair muscle fibres.

Dehydration leads to fatigue and cramping. Before you run ensure you are adequately hydrated; you can do this by checking that your urine is pale and there are large volumes.

When running less than three miles, you should not need to take any water or sports drinks, but this is down to preference. For longer runs, you should take a sports drink in order to replace water and sodium and other minerals lost through sweat.

Preventing injuries

Always take the time to warm up before setting off on a run. Run slowly at first to gradually raise your heart rate, and then do some gentle stretches to loosen yourself up.

After your run you should also 'warm down'. Slow down to a walk to let your heart rate return to normal. This also allows the lactic acid to dissipate and will prevent muscle stiffness. A few stretches will prevent injury and keep you flexible, as running has a habit of tightening your hamstrings.

If you do pick up a minor injury or sprain, a good idea is to remember the acronym R.I.C.E.

R: Rest. Don't run for a few days and try to keep the weight off the injury

I: Ice. Works wonders

C: Compression. A bandage will keep the swelling down

E: Elevation. Raising the injured limb will reduce swelling.

If this does not work, a visit to a physiotherapist is recommended.

Staying safe

- If running solo always tell someone where you are going, especially if you are going off-road, and consider taking a mobile phone
- Wear reflective strips when running at night. A headtorch is only really necessary on unlit country roads
- Invest in waterproofs and look at the weather report before heading into the hills
- Keep the volume on your music as low as possible to ensure you hear approaching vehicles
- Always run facing oncoming traffic
- If a dog bothers you, stay calm and back away slowly, avoiding eye contact or sudden movement.

Starting off

The most common mistake that beginners make is that they start off too fast, resulting in breathlessness which is not fun! Don't put too much pressure on yourself and don't be scared to go slowly or walk – the main aim is to enjoy it. To give you an idea of target speed, you should always be able to talk when running. In saying that, there is no denying that the first few weeks are hard while your body adapts to the new challenges – self-discipline and motivation are essential at this time. It will get easier!

It may help in the early days to follow a programme which combines walking with running:

Week	Session
1	Walk for 2 minutes, then run for 1 minute (repeat 6 times)
2	Walk for 2 minutes and run for 2 minutes (repeat 6 times)
3	Walk for 2 minutes, run for 3 minutes (repeat 6 times)
4	4-minute run, 1-minute walk, 5-minute run, 1-minute walk (repeat 3 times)
5	Run 5 minutes, 1-minute walk, 8-minute run, 1-minute walk, 10-minute run
6	10-minute run, 1-minute walk (repeat 2 times)
7	15 minute run, 2-minute walk, 15-minute run
8	Run for 25 minutes solidly. Keep doing this, increasing the time and/or speed if possible.

After you have completed this beginners' programme, aim to run for 20-30 minutes three times a week.

Tips for beginners

- Start slow: walk if you want to
- Run on scenic routes – it will help motivate you
- Rest between runs
- Buy running clothes that you feel good in – it helps with motivation
- Find a running buddy; this will make it harder to cancel sessions
- If you feel pain in any muscle or joint, stop – don't run through it
- Vary the surface you run on, as it helps to prevent injuries by giving certain muscles and joints a rest, while strengthening others.

Longer, faster

The more you run, the more your strength and stamina will improve. Below are some simple tips to take yourself up a level.

Tips for improvers

- Join a running club for some healthy competition
- Sign up for a race to keep you motivated
- Make a note of all your training sessions including how you felt
- Set realistic short- and long-term goals and keep to them
- Include interval and hill training
- Consider cross training, such as cycling or swimming
- Have a healthy balanced diet to give you the essential nutrients and energy for your training
- Once every two weeks run a familiar route and time yourself, trying to beat your previous time.

Your first race

Races are fun and motivating, and completing one gives a justifiable sense of achievement. There are so many races these days, that if you have been running regularly, sooner or later you will be tempted to test yourself.

Tips for races

- Ease off your training three to four days before the race
- Eat around 200-400 calories two to three hours before the race
- Ensure you are adequately hydrated beforehand
- Get to the race early in order to warm up and prepare yourself
- Avoid wearing new clothes
- Wear a watch to time your race and plan what time you will be at certain distance markers
- Don't start off too fast in all the excitement; this will only cause problems later on
- Bring along family for support
- Eat after the race to replenish glycogen stores
- Stretch afterwards and recover with a few days of light runs.

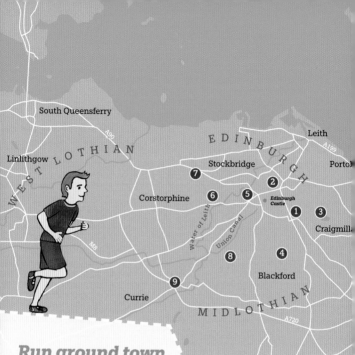

Run around town

Edinburgh's streets are steeped in history. The medieval Old Town's tightly packed closes and wynds contain most of the city's famous tourist sights, while the Georgian neoclassical New Town to the north of Princes Street has a symmetrical layout with broad, straight streets. The benefit of this for runners is a choice of routes with a variety of surfaces, gradients and navigational landmarks – in the shadow of some of Europe's most celebrated architecture.

Through the midst of all this history but far removed from the bustle and traffic, two waterside paths thread their secretive way: the Water of Leith Walkway links Balerno at the foot of the Pentlands with Leith Docks, passing through Colinton Dell, Dean Village and other picturesque destinations on its 20.5km journey; the Union Canal embarks from the heart of Edinburgh to link with

FIRTH OF FORTH

Aberlady

Musselburgh

A1

EAST LOTHIAN

Dalkeith

Glasgow's Forth & Clyde Canal,
51km west at Falkirk. Within the
capital itself, the canal corridor passes
over aqueducts and under bridges
as it makes its journey through
Kingsknowe, Wester Hailes and Ratho.
Both paths are soft surfaced, well
maintained and understandably
popular with runners – and, during
August's back-to-back festivals, come
into their own as a welcome retreat
from the congested city streets.

9

Royal Mile and Arthur's Seat

Time 35 minutes
Distance 5.5km/3.4 miles
Terrain pavement; steady incline
for around 1km
Lights? yes, except on
Queen's Drive

This is a captivating run which
takes you down the historic Royal
Mile, through Holyrood Park, past
the student areas and over
George IV Bridge.

● Start at the top of The Mound
at the corner of Bank Street and
the **Royal Mile**, which runs
between Edinburgh Castle and
Holyrood Palace.

▶ Run down the cobbled Mile, past
the City Chambers on your left. Carry
straight on across both crossroads,
passing the World's End pub and
continuing down the Canongate to
the **Scottish Parliament** building at
the very bottom. At the roundabout,
turn right opposite **Holyrood Palace**.

▶ Follow the road as it bends left and
carries on to the junction with **Queen's
Drive**. Turn right, running uphill for
around 1km on a steady incline which
steepens towards the top.

▶ After the long, sweeping curve
around Salisbury Crags, turn right
at the roundabout, carry on for
around 20m to the next
roundabout and take the last exit
along Holyrood Park Road, past
Edinburgh University Pollock Halls
of Residence and the **Royal
Commonwealth Pool**.

▶ At the T-junction, cross the road
and turn right along **Dalkeith
Road**, then first left onto East
Preston Street. At the crossroads,
go straight on and, at the next
junction, turn right onto
Summerhall Place. Continue
straight on along this as it
becomes **Buccleuch Street** with
the **Meadows** on your left.

▶ **Buccleuch Street** eventually
becomes **Potterrow**, which you
leave to turn right when you reach
Bristo Place. This leads right onto
George IV Bridge which takes you
back to the Royal Mile's High
Street where you started.

10

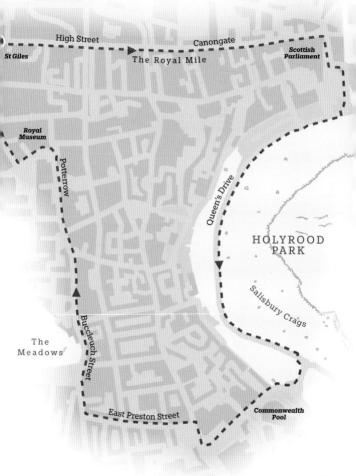

St Giles

High Street

Canongate

The Royal Mile

Scottish
Parliament

Royal
Museum

Potterrow

Queen's Drive

HOLYROOD
PARK

Salisbury Crags

Buccleuch Street

The
Meadows

East Preston Street

Commonwealth
Pool

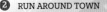

Canonmills

Stockbridge Colonies

Glenogle Road

King George V Park

Henderson Row

Water of Leith

Hamilton Place

Dundas Street

Queen Street Gardens

Queen S

Stockbridge and Calton Hill

Time 45 minutes
Distance 7.2km/4.5 miles
Terrain road and tarmac path; steady climb up Dundas St, shorter inclines at Leith St and Calton Hill
Lights? Yes – although Calton Hill is only lit in parts

This run combines a circuit of bohemian Stockbridge with the city centre's best viewpoint.

● The run starts on the corner of **Broughton Street** and **York Place**. Run down **Broughton Street** and

continue straight on at the roundabout as it becomes Bellevue. Carry straight on at the crossroads to **Canonmills Junction**.

▶ Turn left onto Brandon Terrace and then first right along **Glenogle Road** past the parallel terraces that form the **Stockbridge Colonies**.

▶ Following the road round, enter lively Stockbridge at Deanhaugh Street, with a gentle incline on turning left here. Go straight on over the bridge and, after the first traffic lights,

12

Broughton Street

Picardy Place

Royal Terrace

York Place

St James Centre

Leith Street

Regent Gardens

Calton Hill

Regent Terrace

Regent Road

turn left along **Hamilton Place**; this becomes **Henderson Row**.

▶ At the crossroads, turn right up **Dundas Street**. Turn left onto **Queen Street** (later **York Place**), keeping to the right for an easy right turn at the roundabout, climbing up **Leith Street** with John Lewis on your right.

▶ Cross Leith Street and, at the top, turn left onto Waterloo Place. At Calton Hill, climb the steps on the left, following the sign for Hume Walk. This is a gentle incline with

beautiful Forth views. Where the path splits, follow the right fork uphill.

▶ After the bollards, you join a tarmac road, turning left downhill with views to Arthur's Seat and the Crags. Emerging on **Regent Road**, turn left and keep left to follow Regent, Carlton and **Royal Terrace**s round to the top of Leith Walk.

▶ Turn left and cross to the far side of Leith Walk where **Picardy Place** soon leads you back to Broughton Street.

13

Holyrood and Duddingston

Time 60 minutes
Distance 9.3km/5.8 miles
Terrain road; long inclines around
Arthur's Seat and Dalkeith Road
Lights? none until you reach
Duddingston Village

This circuit takes you beneath the
Crags in Holyrood Park and through
picturesque Duddingston Village.

🔵 Start by **St Margaret's Loch**,
at the bottom of the hill on
Queen's Drive.

▶ Run up the hill beneath the
dramatic **Salisbury Crags**. Turn
right at the roundabout at the top
and first left at the next one to
continue along **Old Church Lane**.

▶ This brings you past
Duddingston Loch and into the
village, now cobbled underfoot,
passing a church on your right.

▶ At the junction with **Duddingston
Road West**, turn left past **Holyrood
High School** and **Duddingston
Golf Course** and carry on to a
crossroads after 1.2km.

▶ Turn right here onto **Milton
Road West** and follow it to the
junction with **Duddingston Park
South**. Go right and then right again
following **Peffermill Road**.

St Margaret's Loch

At Cameron Toll shopping centre turn right up **Dalkeith Road**, following signs for the Old Town. This road is on a slight incline, ideal for speed work, using lamp-posts as markers for alternate sprints and slow jogs.

At the junction after Pollock Halls and the **Royal Commonwealth Pool**, carry straight on – there are now only flats and downhills. Dalkeith Road runs into the **Pleasance**, roughly parallel with Queens Drive.

At the bottom of the hill, turn right onto **Holyrood Road**, passing the Scotsman Building and branching right past **Dynamic Earth**. Continue straight on to reach Queen's Drive and turn left to return to the start.

Duddingston Road West

Duddingston Loch

Holyrood High

Duddingston Golf Course

Milton Road West

tonfield Course

Peffermill Road

Duddingston Park South

15

Marchmont and The Grange

Time 40 minutes
Distance 6.1km/3.8 miles
Terrain road; mainly flat
Lights? yes

This great route takes you through the vibrant student area of Marchmont and past the fine houses of the Grange.

 Start at the **Warrender Park Road/ Marchmont Road** junction, a couple of streets south of The Meadows.

▶ Run west along Warrender Park Road to its end, turning left onto **Whitehouse Lane**.

▶ Reaching the junction with Newbattle Terrace and **Grange Loan**, turn right onto Newbattle Terrace, then first left down **Canaan Lane**.

▶ Take the first left down **Woodburn Terrace** and third left onto **Cluny Gardens,** passing the foot of Blackford Hill where the road soon becomes **Charterhall Road**.

▶ At the crossroads, turn left to head along **Blackford Avenue** till it meets **Grange Loan**, where you turn right and, later, left at **Findhorn Place**.

▶ Take the third left to follow **Grange Road**, and then seventh right onto Kilgraston Road, which leads you onto **Marchmont Road** and back to the start.

Woodburn Terrace

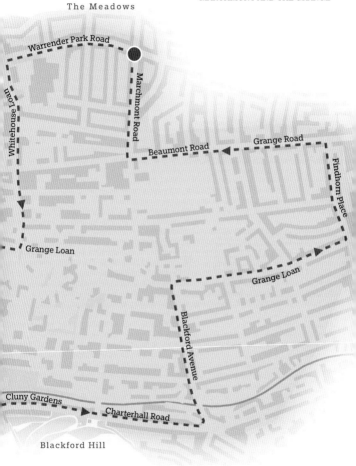

Dean Village and the Water of Leith

Time 30 minutes
Distance 4.6km/2.9 miles
Terrain roads and paths; mostly flat although there are some steps
Lights? none along the Water of Leith

This is a short but beautiful route, which sets out along the Water of Leith from Stockbridge to return beneath the celebrated Georgian architecture of the West End and New Town.

Start at the west end of **Saunders Street** in Stockbridge, where you can access the Water of Leith Walkway.

▶ Head west, following the brown 'To Balerno' signs, with the water on your right. Make sure you look up to admire the spectacular **Dean Bridge** as you pass beneath it, before entering Dean Village, whose eclectic mix of architecture only adds to the charm of this former milling centre.

▶ Head up a gentle incline towards Bell's Brae and cross the road onto Hawthorn Bank Lane. Pass the cottages before heading down the small hill. Cross the bridge at the bottom, making an immediate sharp

18

right on the far side to take you back to the water's edge. Just upstream from Dean Village, pass the – you'll hear it first – and climb the metal steps before continuing along the path.

▶ After crossing back over the water and going up a small ramp, go sharp left and up a flight of more than 100 steps to leave the Water of Leith behind. (For an extra speed/strength training session, run up them two at a time, walk back down, then run up one at a time. Repeat as many times as you can.)

Douglas Crescent

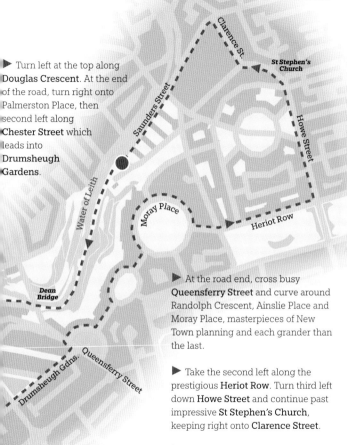

► Turn left at the top along **Douglas Crescent**. At the end of the road, turn right onto Palmerston Place, then second left along **Chester Street** which leads into **Drumsheugh Gardens**.

► At the road end, cross busy **Queensferry Street** and curve around Randolph Crescent, Ainslie Place and Moray Place, masterpieces of New Town planning and each grander than the last.

► Take the second left along the prestigious **Heriot Row**. Turn third left down **Howe Street** and continue past impressive **St Stephen's Church**, keeping right onto **Clarence Street**.

► At the end of the road, turn left onto Hamilton Place, carrying straight on at the traffic lights back to **Saunders Street**.

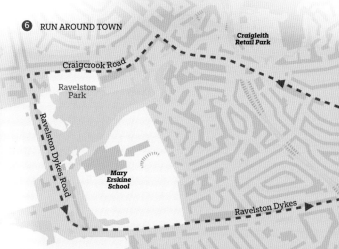

Queensferry Road and Ravelston

Time 45 minutes
Distance 7km/4.4 miles
Terrain road; one steep hill
Lights? yes

This is a nice well-lit circular route in the West End that's good to do in all seasons, but especially in winter when the days are shorter.

🔴 Start on the corner of **Palmerston Place** and **Chester Street**.

▶ Run along **Chester Street** and **Drumsheugh Gardens**, turning left at the T-junction for a long stretch on **Queensferry Road**.

20

▶ This crosses Dean Bridge, passes the impressive **Stewart's Melville College** and continues straight on towards Blackhall at the roundabout and, later, at the **Craigleith Retail Park** junction.

▶ About 300m further on, at the point where there are shops on both sides of the road, turn left onto Craigcrook Place which leads into **Craigcrook Road**. This is a lovely road to run along, passing **Ravelston Park** on your left.

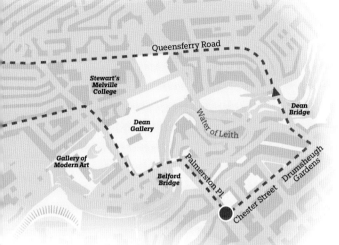

Turn second left onto **Ravelston Dykes Road**, running uphill past the golf course. After 750m, the road flattens out and you pass **Mary Erskine School** on your left.

Continue along **Ravelston Dykes** to the crossroads, with the back of **Stewart's Melville College** ahead on the left.

Turn right onto Belford Road and run downhill past the Dean Gallery and the Gallery of Modern Art and cross the **Belford Bridge**.

Follow the road uphill to the right on Douglas Gardens, which soon leads back onto **Palmerston Place**.

Ravelston and Roseburn

Time 45 minutes
Distance 6.8km/4.2 miles
Terrain tarmac paths and roads;
mainly flat with one long hill
Lights? none on the cyclepath

Set out on the former railway routes
of the Roseburn and Blackhall Paths
for a traffic-free start, then pass the
fine houses of a prestigious
residential area in the run up
towards Ravelston Dykes.

● Start at the bridge on **Ravelston Dykes**, which is on the north side of the road between Garscube Terrace and Orchard Road South.

▶ Follow the path down the side of the bridge, signposted **Roseburn Path**. At the bottom, as you join the cyclepath, turn left.

▶ At a fork after around 1km, keep left to follow **Blackhall Path**, also signposted Davidson Mains, to a junction after around 1.6km. Keep right here – do not go under the bridge. At the top of the short incline, the path ends.

▶ Turn left onto Silverknowes Drive and first left again at Silverknowes Terrace, following signs for National Cycle Route 1 – the main northbound cycle route out of Edinburgh.

▶ After around 200m, turn left to emerge on Cramond Road South. Go left here, carrying straight on when you reach the roundabout to join **Quality Street**, passing the church on your right.

▶ As you approach the Quality Street Junction, continue straight on to **Craigcrook Road**.

Quality Street

Hillhouse Road

Craigcrook Road

Blackhall Path

▶ Turn right up **Ravelston Dykes Road** – this is a steep, relentless hill. Pass **Ravelston Golf Cours**e on your right and carry on to the top. Continue straight on at the traffic lights and back to the bridge where you started.

Craigleith Retail Park

Ravelston Park

Ravelston Dykes Road

Roseburn Path

lston Course

Mary Erskine School

Ravelston Dykes

The Union Canal and Craiglockhart

Time 50 minutes

Distance 8.2km/5.1 miles

Terrain road and pathway; hill at Craiglockhart Avenue leads to another incline up Glenlockhart Road

Lights? none on the Union Canal

A delightful route, following the peaceful canal corridor from its start at Lochrin Basin and returning via Craiglockhart and Morningside.

🔴 Start at **Fountainbridge** off Lothian Road. Just by the roundabout, you'll see a cobbled street.

▶ Take this street to reach the start of the **Union Canal**. With the water on your left, the towpath leads past the Leamington Lift Bridge and **Harrison Park East**, under a bridge and on past Harrison Park West.

▶ After running under two bridges in quick succession (the first numbered 4a) and passing **Meggetland** on your right, you come to a metal bridge and, to its right, steps leaving the canal.

▶ Climb these, turning left at the top to cross the bridge and follow a gently rising path. At the top, turn right onto Craiglockhart Road North and then left at the top of the road to run uphill on Craiglockhart Avenue.

▶ At the crossroads, continue straight up past **Napier University**, where the street name changes to **Glenlockhart Road**. This is a lovely road to run, passing **Merchants of Edinburgh Golf Course** and Craiglockhart Hill.

▶ Continue to **Greenbank Drive** and, at the main **Comiston Road**, turn left down the hill towards Morningside. Stay on this road for around 1.6km as it becomes **Morningside Road** and then **Bruntsfield Place**, passing Bruntsfield Links on your right.

▶ Take the next left to drop down **Leamington Terrace** and cross Gilmore Place to briefly follow Leamington Road, before crossing the canal. Turn right along the wide cobbled area and back to the start.

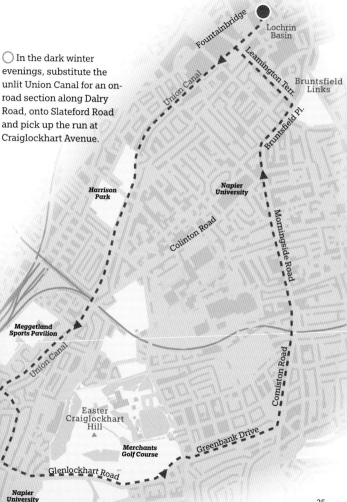

In the dark winter evenings, substitute the unlit Union Canal for an on-road section along Dalry Road, onto Slateford Road and pick up the run at Craiglockhart Avenue.

Lochrin Basin

Fountainbridge

Leamington Terr.

Bruntsfield Links

Bruntsfield Pl.

Union Canal

Harrison Park

Napier University

Morningside Road

Colinton Road

Meggetland Sports Pavilion

Union Canal

Easter Craiglockhart Hill

Merchants Golf Course

Comiston Road

Greenbank Drive

Glenlockhart Road

Napier University

25

The Water of Leith

Time 2 hours
Distance 20.5km/12.7 miles
Terrain mainly flat, pathways and some roads
Lights? none on the Water of Leith

The Water of Leith rises in the Pentland Hills and empties into the Firth of Forth at the Port of Leith, passing through some of the capital's most interesting suburbs and city villages along the way. By tackling the walkway in its entirety, you can appreciate the slow, unfolding transformation from rolling moorland to bustling port.

🔴 Start at the beginning of the **Water of Leith Walkway**, just off Bridge Road by the High School in Balerno.

▶ The first part of this route is easy to navigate – just follow the brown Water of Leith signs, as the walkway travels through **Currie** and **Juniper Green**, and then on through **Colinton Dell** and **Kingsknowe**.

A70

CURRIE

Water of Leith

BALERNO

HMP Saughton

● **SLATEFORD**

► Cross **Slateford Road** to the Water of Leith Visitor Centre, and continue along the Water of Leith, to emerge onto and cross **Gorgie Road**.

Colinton Dell

Merchiston School

WESTER HAILES

City Bypass

JUNIPER GREEN

○ This is a great run if you are training for a marathon; as the terrain is fairly soft and flat, there is a low risk of injury. Buses run direct from the city centre to Balerno – the route can be run in either direction.

▶ The Water of Leith signs lead you on to **Ford's Road**, where more signs (also for Saughton Sports Complex) send you right and then first left, passing through gateposts and following the path round.

▶ Cross **Balgreen Road** and go straight through the gates so the Water of Leith is on your right.

▶ Turn first right over the bridge, following the sign for Leith, with the path now leading through **Roseburn Park**. Turn left at the end of the path (signed) and take the first left along **Roseburn Gardens**.

▶ Turn right on **Roseburn Terrace** and then first left, following the signs leading down the steps back to the Water of Leith.

▶ In Dean Village, at the end of this path, turn left and double back on yourself over the bridge. Turn left to keep going up the cobbled hill. Continue straight over at the crossroads along **Miller Row** and then under the **Dean Bridge**.

Royal Botanic Gardens

STOCKBRIDGE

Dean Gallery

Gallery of Modern Art

Water of Leith

Roseburn Park

HAYMARKET

Murrayfield Stadium

GORGIE

▶ Continue along the path until you reach some steps – turn right onto **Glenogle Road**, passing the charming **Stockbridge Colonies**.

▶ Take a left down **Bell Place**, cross the bridge and turn right at the bottom. This will bring you out at **Inverleith Terrace Lane**.

▶ Turn right at the end of the road onto **Inverleith Row**, cross this road and, after the bridge, take **Warriston Road** to your left.

▶ At the end of this stretch, turn left and run down steps, then right under a bridge and along **Saunders Street**.

▶ Now in **Stockbridge**, cross at the crossroads and turn left over the bridge, taking the steps immediately to the right of the bridge back to the water's edge.

▶ Run under a bridge, follow the road round over **St Mark's Bridge** and descend the steps immediately to the right. The rest is easy – follow the walkway all the way to Leith.

29

Parklife

Edinburgh has 144 parks and almost 1500 hectares of parkland and green space – from its very heart out to the city limits and beyond. It's little wonder that it is regarded as one of the most beautiful cities in the world.

For the runner, this abundance of parkland is a double blessing. Although there is much to be enjoyed in running along Edinburgh's streets, alternating this with an escape from the traffic and crowds keeps things interesting. Changing the surface you run on is also so important in preventing injuries and strengthening other muscles and joints. Some of the best road routes will mix running on grass paths with running on the pavement – this chapter includes a selection of these.

Once you have mastered running on the level, incorporating hills into your route provides resistance training, which helps strengthen your legs and improve general aerobic capacity. Many of Edinburgh's hilly parks provide an ideal training ground for starting hill running.

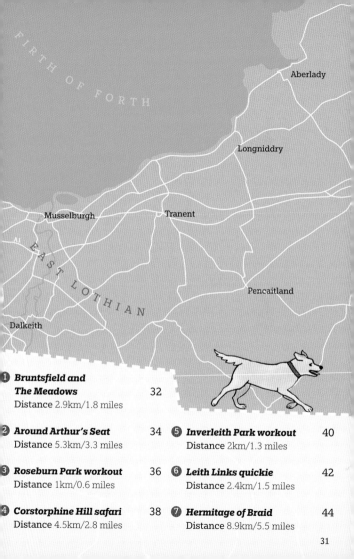

FIRTH OF FORTH

Aberlady

Longniddry

Musselburgh   Tranent

EAST LOTHIAN

Pencaitland

Dalkeith

Bruntsfield and The Meadows

Time 20 minutes
Distance 2.9km/1.8 miles
Terrain path and road; flat
with one small hill
Lights? yes

The Meadows is a large park
situated to the south of the
city and is well used by
runners and walkers. This
run is good for beginners as
it is mainly flat, and also
allows you to alternate
walking and running until
your fitness improves.

Brougham Place

Lonsdale Drive

Leven Terrace

Melville Drive

BRUNTSFIELD
LINKS

Leamington Walk

Warrender Park Terrace

● Start at **Melville Drive** at the
junction with **Marchmont Road**.

▶ Turn right and run along the path
on the perimeter of **the Meadows**.

▶ At the end, by the playpark, follow
the path round to the left. Keep
following the path round the park, till
you reach **Brougham Place**.

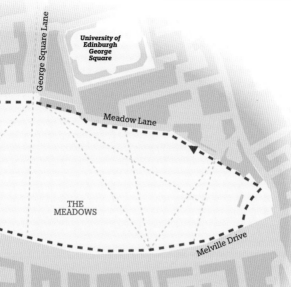

► Cross this road to **Leven Terrace**, leave the road and run up **Bruntsfield Links**, where there is a small hill. Follow the path to the right.

► If you wish you can use this hill for some sprint work. Sprint up the hill for about 50m and walk back down. Repeat four times – increasing the distance and number of repetitions as you progress.

► Carry on up the hill and turn left at the top. Run down **Leamington Walk** before turning left onto **Marchmont Road** at the bottom to return to the start.

Around Arthur's Seat

Time 35 minutes
Distance 5.3km/3.3 miles
Terrain road; one very steep hill, then a nice downhill to compensate
Lights? none, except at the roundabouts

Arthur's Seat is an extinct volcano and the main peak in the group of hills that form Holyrood Park, at the heart of the city. This is a run that you must do at some point – the views are fantastic and the terrain as rugged as any small hill in the Highlands, but be warned, it is a tough climb!

🔴 This run starts at the car park at Holyrood Palace to follow **Queen's Drive**, which circumnavigates Arthur's Seat.

▶ Turn left from the car park and run along **Queen's Drive** for around 600m, before turning right just after **St Margaret's Loch** – avoiding the swans!

▶ Follow the road up the steep, winding hill, with views to East Lothian on your left.

▶ After a relentless 1.3km of climbing, as you approach **Dunsapie Loch**, it levels out. Enjoy the flatter surface and the great views to the Pentland Hills.

▶ The road starts to go downhill towards a roundabout – keep following the hill straight down, with **Arthur's Seat** on your right.

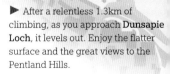

Our Dynamic Earth

HOLYROOD PARK

Salisbury Crags

Queen's Drive

St Margaret's Loch

Dunsaple Loch

Arthur's Seat

Crow Hill

Queen's Drive

► To the right of the road there is a grassy area ideal for hill running. A sample session is as follows: walk downhill for around 60m, turn round and run back to the start;

walk back down and repeat four times, increasing the distance and number of repetitions as you improve.

► From here, keep following **Queen's Drive** back round to the start.

Roseburn Park workout

Time 40 minutes
Distance 1km/0.6 miles
Terrain grass; flat
Lights? no

Roseburn Park is an ideal training ground for mixing speed work and plyometrics because it is flat, and the trees around the perimeter are a useful gauge of distance – as well as providing rain shelter if required! This training is great for improving speed, power, co-ordination and agility. As the exercises put a huge amount of stress on your body, however, it is recommended that you are reasonably fit before trying out this session.

Roseburn Park is next to the Water of Leith by **Murrayfield Stadium**. It can be accessed by Murrayfield Ice Rink or by either end of **Roseburn Crescent**.

▶ Make sure you warm up properly by jogging round the park at least twice. Alternatively, as Roseburn Park is in the city centre, you could run here to warm up.

▶ Run round the park, sprinting for 100 steps and then jogging for 100 to get your breath back. Repeat this until you have run round the park twice. Have a five-minute walk to recover and repeat the above.

▶ The plyometric session now begins. Find a nice flat area and carry out the following exercises:

• Hopping: Hop on your left leg for 20 steps, raising your lifted knee as far as possible. Walk back to your start point and then hop on your right leg for 20 steps.

• Squat Jump: Stand with your feet shoulder width apart, bend your knees in a squat position and using your arms jump forward as far as you can; on landing, immediately start the next jump. Do 10 of these, then walk back to the start.

• Lunge Jump: Start in the lunge position, jump up and land in the same lunge position; repeat this 10 times then change legs and repeat.

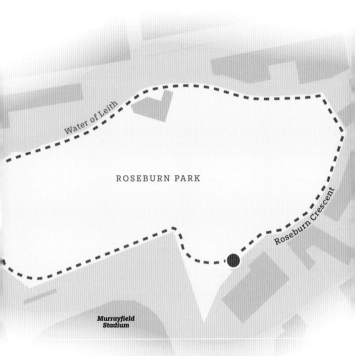

- Double Leg Jumps: Stand with feet slightly apart, explosively jump straight up and pull your knees to your chest. Repeat 10 times.

- Have a five-minute break and then repeat all the exercises. The aim should be to repeat these sets of exercises four times.

◯ **Any other flat park will do for this workout – Inverleith Park, Holyrood Park, The Meadows and Leith Links are all ideal.**

Corstorphine Hill safari

Time 30 minutes
Distance 4.5km/2.8 miles
Terrain dirt paths, rocky in parts;
one hill at start and one at the end
Lights? no

This short route round Corstorphine
Hill, a public park and nature
reserve to the west of Edinburgh, is
challenging but has fantastic views
of the city. You can even catch a
glimpse of some of the animals in
Edinburgh Zoo!

CORSTORPHINE
HILL LOCAL
NATURE
RESERVE

Corstorphine
Hill

Clermiston Road

Hillwood
House

Cairnmuir Road

⬤ Start on the public footpath
just off **Ravelston Dykes Road**,
between Ravelston Dykes Lane
and Murrayfield Road
(signed Corstorphine Hill).

▶ Follow the path up the hill, which
is gradual to start, before steepening
to a sharp incline. After around 600m,
the path narrows. On a good day, the
views from here are great.

▶ Carry on up the narrower path for
around 100m to a bench and
crossroads of paths by a wall. Turn
right and continue uphill until you
pass the radio mast.

► Now run down some steps to a path junction. Turn right and take the more level path that contours the side of the hill, again offering beautiful views over the city.

There are various little paths that leave the main trail, but stick to this one. A larger path joins you to the right. Continue straight on, following the path down to the left to reach **Clermiston Road**.

► Stay on the grassy area parallel to the road, crossing the drive for the General Teaching Council for Scotland, until the grass ends and you find yourself on Clermiston Road.

► Take the first left onto **Cairnmuir Road** (SP Corstorphine Hill).

► Re-enter the park where the road ends. Keep right at the junction of paths and climb the steps towards the mast once more.

► Follow the path back round the hill, turning left after the wall, and drop down the steep slope to the start.

Ravelston Dykes Road

Ravelston
Golf Course

Edinburgh Zoo

Inverleith Park workout

Time 13 minutes
Distance 2km/1.3 miles
Terrain grassy paths and tarmac;
one small hill
Lights? lights in some areas

Situated to the north of the city next to the Royal Botanic Garden, Inverleith Park is a beautiful well-equipped green space, perfect for a quick run after a long day at the office. It is also ideal for beginners who can mix running with walking, measuring their progress by how many circuits they achieve.

You should also check out a recent addition to the park – an excellent fitness trail on the north side which features 10 stations, including tyre runs and benches for sit-ups.

🔴 Start at one of the entrances to Inverleith Park, about midway along **Inverleith Place**. The park is split length- and breadthways by two tarmac paths, with a dirt path round the perimeter.

▶ After entering the park at the gates, turn right along the perimeter path, pass the **allotments** on your left and continue.

East Fettes Avenue

▶ Cross the tarmac path and carry on downhill. At the bottom, turn left on the second path, passing the **pond** on your left, and then turn left up the small incline before turning first right.

▶ Run past the children's play area and then turn left past the tennis courts, following the path parallel to **Arboretum Place**.

▶ Turn left at the bottom to return to the start point.

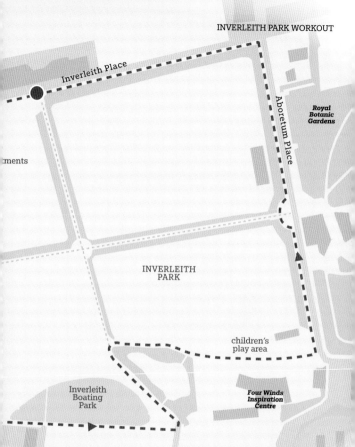

Inverleith Place

Aboretum Place

Royal
Botanic
Gardens

ments

INVERLEITH
PARK

children's
play area

Inverleith
Boating
Park

Four Winds
Inspiration
Centre

○ For an alternative training session, use the northeast quadrant bounded by Inverleith Place and Arboretum Place. Sprint the length of one side of the square, jog the next length, sprint the next length and jog back to your start point. Repeat after a five-minute rest. Then sprint one length of the quadrant and jog the diagonal to recover – repeat this four times.

41

Leith Links quickie

Time 15 minutes
Distance 2.4km/1.5 miles
Terrain grassy path; flat
Lights? yes

The main area of open space in the capital's harbour area was levelled in 1888 when it became a public park extending to 46 acres. As a result, it makes the ideal short, flat route for beginners. There is easy parking and no navigation difficulties on this simple run around the tree-lined perimeter.

John's place
Links Place
Duncan Place
Links Gardens
LEITH LINKS WEST
Hermitage Place
East Hermitage Place

● Start at the junction of **Links Gardens**, which slices the park in two, and **Gladstone Place**.

▶ Run east, parallel with **Claremont Park**, following the perimeter of the park.

▶ Cross Links Gardens to the other side of the park. Keep to the right, parallel to **Links Place**, turning left at its junction with **John's Place**.

▶ Continue heading up the park towards **East Hermitage Place** and along the perimeter back to the start.

○ This circuit can be completed in either direction, as many times as you can comfortably manage.

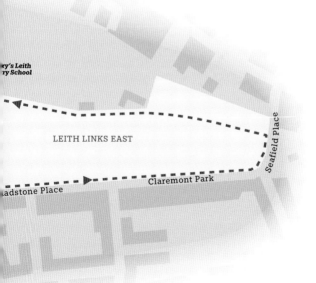

ry's Leith
ry School

LEITH LINKS EAST

Gladstone Place

Claremont Park

Seafield Place

Hermitage of Braid

Time 60 minutes
Distance 8.9km/5.5miles
Terrain rocky paths and roads; long steep hill at Howe Dean which continues to the Braid Hills bridle-path; nice downhills to compensate
Lights? no

This circular route runs through the wooded Hermitage of Braid Nature Reserve before emerging onto open hill. There is one main steep climb, but the views from the top make it worthwhile.

🔵 Start at the Hermitage of Braid Nature Reserve car park off Midmar Drive.

▶ Pass through the gate and follow the muddy trail to the left to join the path curving to the right around Blackford Hill. Take care with your footing – it descends quite steeply.

▶ Go down the steps and keep left, following the path by the **Braid Burn** for around 400m.

▶ As the surface turns to gravel, bear right over the bridge to the narrow **Howe Dean Path**. This gives a long, steep climb; walk if necessary.

▶ At the top, emerge onto **Braid Hills Drive**, turning left to run down the road for around 500m, then right onto the red shale **Braid Hills bridlepath**. It's a fairly long climb to reach the phonemasts at the top, but you are rewarded with a fantastic view over Edinburgh.

▶ The path narrows to descend the hill – take care with your footing. Keeping to the left, the track will eventually bring you out by **Mortonhall Club House**.

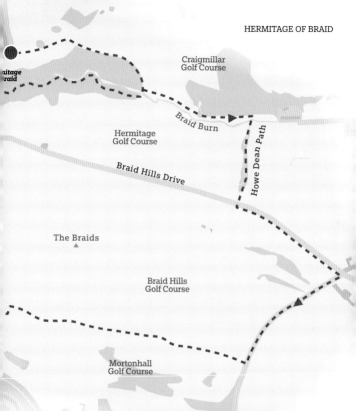

Craigmillar
Golf Course

Braid Burn

Hermitage
Golf Course

Howe Dean Path

Braid Hills Drive

The Braids

Braid Hills
Golf Course

Mortonhall
Golf Course

▶ Cross the road and turn right. Take the first left onto **Riselaw Crescent** and follow this round until you come to **Comiston Road**.

▶ Turn right and continue downhill to the crossroads, turn right and run past the church onto **Braidburn Terrace**.

▶ At the roundabout, turn right onto **Braid Road** and then re-enter the Hermitage of Braid Nature Reserve.

▶ Follow the path till you come to a large bridge on the right, and turn left up the last hill (you descended this at the start) towards the car park.

East coast and country parks

If you need a change to your regular route to fire your mojo, you can't do much better than this selection of runs to the east of the city centre, all within easy reach by bus or car.

No coverage of the east would be complete, of course, without featuring the famous Edinburgh and East Lothian coastline, and this chapter highlights three of the best beach runs – Portobello Promenade, just minutes from the city centre, dune-fringed Gullane Bay and popular Yellowcraigs.

Inland from Portobello and Musselburgh, in Midlothian, you'll also discover two of Edinburgh's finest country parks, with two very different runs to familiarise you with accessible Dalkeith Country Park and one, further out, at Vogrie Estate.

Finally, there is a chance to glimpse the area's mining heritage as you cross from the Midlothian to East Lothian countryside on the popular Pencaitland Railway Path.

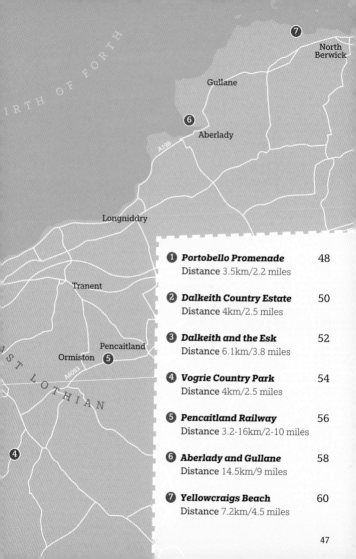

North Berwick

Gullane

FIRTH OF FORTH

⑥

Aberlady

A198

Longniddry

Tranent

Pencaitland

Ormiston ⑤

A6093

EAST LOTHIAN

④

⑦

Portobello Promenade

Time 25 minutes
Distance 3.5km/2.2 miles
Terrain flat tarmac path,
pedestrianised
Lights? yes

This flat run is great for beginners,
as well as for more advanced
runners looking for a speed session.

48

Start at the corner of **King's Road**
and King's Place in Portobello.

▶ This is an easy route to follow.
Simply set out along the **promenade**
and return the same way. To make a
circuit of it, you can run back along
Joppa Road, but being next to the sea
is so much nicer.

▶ Turn right along the promenade, or take to the sand if you prefer a more challenging workout.

▶ With views out to East Lothian on a clear day, pass the Portobello Indoor Bowls and **Leisure Centre**.

▶ Continue past Portobello Swim Centre, to the end of the promenade where it meets **Joppa Road**. Turn round and return the same way, this time with views of Fife.

◯ There are streetlights all the way along the promenade, which is great for beginners and runners looking to improve their speed. A beginner can alternate running between two lampposts with walking. Alternatively, you can sprint between two lampposts and recover by jogging between two.

Portobello Promenade

Portobello Beach

Bedford Terrace

Joppa Road

Dalkeith Country Estate

Time 25 minutes
Distance 4km/2.5 miles
Terrain tarmac and muddy paths;
a few small inclines
Lights? no

Just 8km from the city centre,
Dalkeith Country Estate has 500
acres of woodland and miles of
trails to explore: this run will
help you get your bearings.
There is a small charge in
summer from 8am to 5pm.

DALKEITH
COUNTRY
PARK

🔵 Start at the car park at
the entrance to the country estate,
just off the high street by **St Mary's
Church** in Dalkeith.

▶ Enter the park through the large
gates, with St Mary's Church on your
right. Where the road splits, keep
right along the path that leads down
towards the **adventure playground**.

▶ Immediately after the playground,
turn left towards **Dalkeith House**,
now home to hundreds of North
American Students who study there.

▶ As the road forks, keep right to
soon cross the impressive **Montagu
Bridge**. Keep on this path until you
see a house and large gates ahead.

▶ Just before you reach the gates,
branch off to the left. Continue on
this trail, ignoring the many paths
which leave and join it.

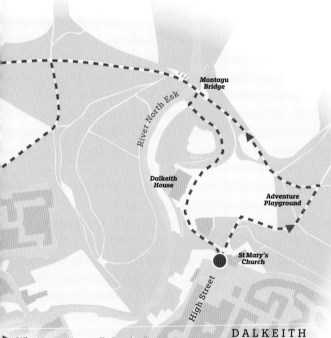

▶ Where you see a wall ahead, veer left with the path, to rejoin your original trail and turn right to return to Montagu Bridge.

▶ Take the first road to the right after the bridge, and pass the front of Dalkeith House, continuing uphill to spy St Mary's Church again. Turn right to return to the start.

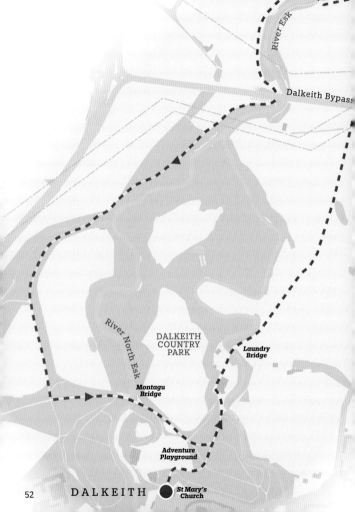

River Esk

Dalkeith Bypass

River North Esk

DALKEITH
COUNTRY
PARK

Laundry
Bridge

Montagu
Bridge

Adventure
Playground

St Mary's
Church

DALKEITH

Dalkeith and the Esk

Time 40 minutes
Distance 6.1km/3.8 miles
Terrain tarmac and muddy paths; mainly flat with a few inclines
Lights? no

● Begin at the car park at the entrance to the country estate, just off the high street by **St Mary's Church** in Dalkeith.

▶ After entering the park through the gates, run along the main tarmac path, passing the **adventure playground** on your left.

▶ Continue straight on and enjoy a downhill over **Laundry Bridge**.

▶ Continue along this road, on a slight incline, until the road splits. Take the road to the left, then first right down a hill and over a small bridge.

▶ Take the dirt track road to the left, doubling back on yourself. This track leads to a junction where you go left downhill and under a large roadbridge. Follow this road round and up the slight incline.

▶ Keep left to follow the trail – you will cross a small burn – then run up a hill, always keeping to the main path.

▶ When you come to the crossroads, turn left, cross **Montagu Bridge** and continue along the path till you are past the adventure playground.

▶ Turn right here and return along the outward road to the start.

Vogrie Country Park

Time 25 minutes
Distance 4km/2.5 miles
Terrain Woodland paths; two steep hills
Lights? no

This is a beautiful run through an old Victorian Estate, west of Gorebridge, 19km from the city centre. There is a charge for parking, but it is free after 6pm.

⚫ Start from the car park and head towards the road (**B6372**) that you came in on. Turn right onto the path that runs parallel with the road.

▶ You will come to a signpost for **Vogrie House**, where you will see a path to the left, signposted Tyne Valley – follow this downhill.

▶ At the bottom of the hill, cross the bridge and turn left, following the sign for Tyne Valley.

▶ You will cross two bridges before climbing a steep hill. Keep to this path, following signs for Alderdean. After crossing a bridge, keep straight, following signs for **Vogrie House** via Alderdean. Carry on over some wooden slats and up another steep hill.

▶ After crossing a bridge, follow the path round to the left, signposted **Vogrie House**.

▶ Where the path splits, keep left to emerge at the side of **Vogrie House**, a hugely impressive baronial mansion.

▶ Follow the signs for the Rhododendron Walk, past the **orchard** and back to the car park.

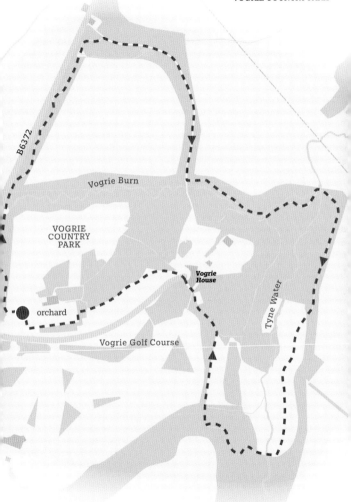

B6372

Vogrie Burn

VOGRIE
COUNTRY
PARK

orchard

Vogrie
House

Tyne Water

Vogrie Golf Course

Pencaitland Railway

Time 20 minutes to 1 hour 40
Distance 3.2–16km/2–10 miles
(round-trip)
Terrain compacted shale; mainly
flat with some gentle inclines
Lights? no

Following the course of the old line
from Pencaitland to Crossgatehall,
near Cousland, the Pencaitland
Railway Walk is ideal both for
beginners and more advanced
runners as you can make your
target two miles or ten!

The railway was originally built to
serve the various mines dotted
along its length and is mostly level.
The surface is good and there are no
navigation difficulties – what's more
the path gives wonderful views of
the countryside as it crosses from
East Lothian to Midlothian.

Crossgatehall

COUSLAND

⬤ Start on **Huntlaw Road** in Pencaitland, just before you go under the old railway bridge, which is around 400m from the village going towards Glenkinchie Distillery.

▶ You will see steps up the side of the bridge. Climb these and turn right along the disused railway.

▶ You can make it your objective to run all the way to **Crossgatehall**, which is 8km one-way. Or carry on as far as you like, then turn back along the same route.

MISTON

PENCAITLAND

Aberlady and Gullane

Time 1 hour 30
Distance 14.5km/9 miles
Terrain woodland paths which can be muddy in parts; a few inclines, but mainly flat
Lights? no

This is a beautiful route combining a blast along the seafront with an inland run along the John Muir Way.

🅿 Start at the car park by **Aberlady Bay** Local Nature Reserve on the coast road just east of Aberlady.

▶ Cross the bridge and follow the trail towards the shore, passing through a pleasant tunnel of trees.

▶ Just after the track becomes a grassy path, you come to a T-junction where you head left towards the sea. Arthur's Seat is in view to the left.

▶ Just before the beach, the path climbs a large sand dune. This is ideal for practising short hill runs (run up and walk down three to four times).

▶ Turn right at the beach and bear northeast towards **Gullane** – there are many paths to vary your run, but if you keep the sea as near to your left as possible, you can't go wrong.

▶ You will eventually come to the beautiful sandy **Gullane Bay** where you can at last take to the beach: keep to the hard sand as the soft stuff is very hard to run in.

▶ At the end of the sand, carry on along the shore path, turning right when you see a small ruin. This path leads around the forest, with many return options to the start – stick to the main one for the easiest navigation.

▶ Instead of returning all the way to the car park, follow the path to **Marine Terrace**, cross the road and run along **Sandy Loan** which brings you to **Gullane** village centre.

▶ Turn left, then second right onto Saltcoats Road. At the end of this road, you will see a green sign for the **John Muir Way**, which takes you past **Luffness Links** on your right, through a gate and onto the road back to the start.

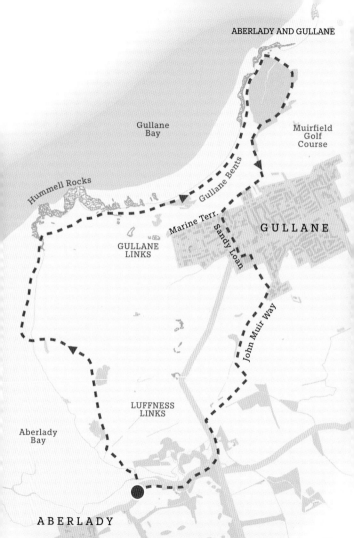

Gullane Bay

Muirfield Golf Course

Hummell Rocks

Gullane Bents

Marine Terr.

GULLANE

GULLANE LINKS

Sandy Loan

John Muir Way

LUFFNESS LINKS

Aberlady Bay

ABERLADY

Yellowcraigs Beach

Time 45 minutes
Distance 7.2km/4.5 miles
Terrain dirt paths, sand; flat
Lights? only in Dirleton

This is a fantastic beachside route which starts and finishes in the village of Dirleton, mostly following the John Muir Way. It's best to wear long trousers and sleeves as there are prickly bushes!

● Start at Manse Road in **Dirleton**, where you pick up the 73km **John Muir Way**, linking East Lothian with Edinburgh and the Scottish Borders.

▶ A dirt road leads you through the fields. Where the path splits, keep to the left (SP John Muir Way, Yellowcraigs). You will be aiming for the treeline, where the path veers to the right.

▶ Take the path to the left over the small bridge, and turn immediately right (SP John Muir Way). This takes you past the **car park** for Yellowcraigs Beach.

Archerfield
Golf Course

Wave ?

John Muir Way

DIRLETON

Dirleton
Castle

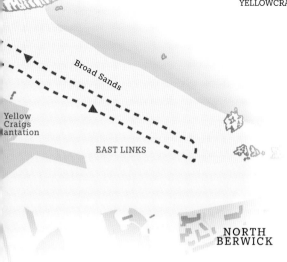

► Joining the main path, turn left (SP John Muir Way).

► Turn right just after the forest (SP John Muir Way). Leave the Way after this and cross diagonally towards the beach, now choosing from numerous paths to keep the beach to your left (beware of prickly bushes!).

► On reaching the golf course, the run takes you onto the sand dunes between the beach and the course.

► As you near various houses on your far right, look out for the wooden bridge by the shore. Cross this to return the way you came, this time back up the beach.

► Approaching the lighthouse on Fidra Island to your right, take the wide path on your left to reluctantly leave the sea behind and return to the outward path.

► Pass the car park at Yellowcraigs and turn right (SP John Muir Way) to return to the start.

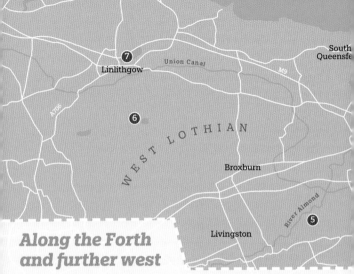

South Queensfe

Linlithgow

Union Canal

M9

WEST LOTHIAN

Broxburn

River Almond

Livingston

Along the Forth and further west

The Firth of Forth is undoubtedly one of Edinburgh's best natural resources for outdoors lovers, providing shoreline runs that not only put a spring in your step and a breeze through your hair, but also give continual interest, whether its the sight offshore of boats, defence artefacts or, if you're lucky, basking seals, or on-land the settlements and estates that cling to it.

While it may not boast the sandy beaches of East Lothian, the Inner Firth to the west of the city centre provides miles of fantastic, sometimes more sheltered shoreline,

with the promenade from Granton to lovely Cramond village proving one of the city's most popular and accessible weekend runs.

For those who are still powered up once they reach Cramond (and if you're not you'll find a cosy nook for refreshment here), there's a satisfying 12.7km circuit to be had by turning inland on the River Almond Walkway.

Further out, the Shore Walk through the Dalmeny Estate from South Queensferry marks the start of another great windswept circuit along the Forth, while back within the city limits, Cammo Estate

provides a wilder, more secluded experience with ruins, architectural curiosities and trees galore.

Out of town in West Lothian, two country parks stand out as offering excellent varied runs – Beecraigs with its loch, plantations and deer farm and Almondell with its woodland and river runs.

Finally, though it is this West Lothian town's most obvious local run, Linlithgow Loch has such a unique combinaton of scenery and accessibility, great for beginners especially, that it warrants a place in this selection.

Cramond seafront

Time 40 minutes
Distance 6km/3.7 miles
Terrain wide tarmac path; flat, may be breezy
Lights? no

It is difficult to believe you are so near town on this beautiful seaside run, despite the overhead reminders that you're on a busy flight path and countless scooters, trikes and walkers on sunny weekends. Navigation is a doddle and beginners can build up to the full route to Cramond.

🔵 Start on **West Shore Road**, about 600m northeast of its junction with **Marine Drive**, in Granton. You will see the white gates barring traffic from the paths.

▶ Take the tarmac path leading directly down to the seafront. On reaching the promenade, turn left and follow the path by the sea. On a clear day, there are fantastic views to Fife and the Forth Bridges.

▶ When you join another path, keep heading right, following the signs for **Cramond**. Look straight ahead and you'll see Cramond Island with the concrete pylons of the causeway leading into the shore: aim for this.

CRAMOND

Silverknowes

Continue straight past the building immediately to your left with triangular shapes on the roof. There is a good grassy slope just past this building if you want to practise some hill running.

In **Cramond**, when you come to a grassy roundabout at the end of the promenade, turn round and head back along the path to the start.

◯ The 5km Edinburgh parkrun is held every Saturday at 9.30am on the Cramond-Silverknowes promenade. It's free, but register to join (parkrun.org.uk).

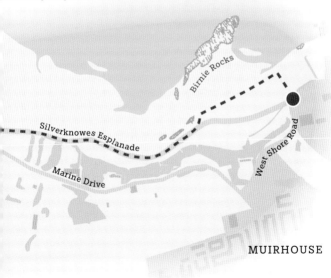

Birnie Rocks

Silverknowes Esplanade

Marine Drive

West Shore Road

MUIRHOUSE

Cramond and Almond

Time 1 hour 20 minutes
Distance 12.7km/7.9 miles
Terrain tarmac and dirt paths;
mainly flat with one incline at
Brae Park Road
Lights? only in limited sections

Begin with a blast of sea air on this
popular Firth of Forth run from
Granton, retreat to the wooded River
Almond Walkway and return on
pavements along National Cycle
Network Route 1 to the promenade.

▶ Start on **West Shore Road**, about
600m northeast of its junction with
Marine Drive, in Granton. You will see
the white gates barring traffic from
the paths.

▶ For an enjoyable
seaside run, follow
the esplanade
until it enters
Cramond
village.

▶ At this point, take the tarmac
path to the left, keeping the **River
Almond** on your right at all times and
following the sign for Cramond
Bridge. This passes the Cramond
Boat Club and leads onto the River
Almond Walkway (be respectful of
other users on this narrower
walkway).

CRAMOND

River Almond

Whitehouse Road

Barnton Avenue West

Brae Park Road

Royal Burgess
Golf Course

Ba

► Pass a ruin on your right and a waterfall. Climb some steps and keep right at the junction, following the river. Run up steep steps, along a flat path and down more steps.

► Pass the houses on your left at Dowies Mill Lane. This will then take you out at **Brae Park Road**, where you turn left to reach its junction with **Whitehouse Road**.

► Continue straight over to **Barnton Avenue West** and carry on along the path between Bruntsfield Links and the **Royal Burgess Golf Course** to reach **Barnton Avenue East**.

Silverknowes Esplanade

West Shore Road

Marine Drive

Silverknowes Road

Silverknowes Golf Course

Lauriston Farm Road

Cramond Road South

enue East

► Carry on along this road to emerge at the Quality Street Junction. Turn left down **Cramond Road South** and second right down **Lauriston Farm Road**.

► At the roundabout, take the first left along **Silverknowes Road**, heading back towards the seafront.

► On reaching the next roundabout, cross over and turn right to find a path to the shore on your left. This takes you back to the promenade, where you retrace your steps to the start.

Cammo runway

Time 20 minutes
Distance 3.4km/2.1 miles
Terrain woodland paths which can be muddy in parts; a few inclines but mainly flat
Lights? no

Though once a planned pleasure ground for early 18th-century aristocrats, the mix of mature woods and grassland that now form much of the 85-acre Cammo Estate create a haven for runners who like more natural parkland. See if you can spot the architectural clues to its illustrious past as you navigate your way round its many paths.

● Start at the car park just off **Cammo Walk**.

▶ Take the path to the right (SP visitor centre 470m). This takes you through the trees and over a small bridge to reach the visitor centre, housed in a former gatehouse.

▶ Turn left onto the main path which is on a slight uphill incline.

▶ After around 100m, take the path branching off to the right and go through the gate into the field. On the right you will see the old Cammo Farm House.

▶ Follow the path as it goes round to the left and climbs slightly uphill – this can be muddy.

▶ At the top of the incline various paths meet: take the path to the right, and, as you come to the treeline, take the path to the left.

▶ Keep on this main path – you will be parallel to the road and then the golf course – and continue as it narrows and enters a field.

▶ On meeting a fence, follow the path to the left, keeping the fence on your right. Eventually this brings you out at the top of a small hill, where you will see the **watertower** straight ahead.

▶ Run down the hill past the watertower. Just before you come to a derelict building, turn right to return to the car park.

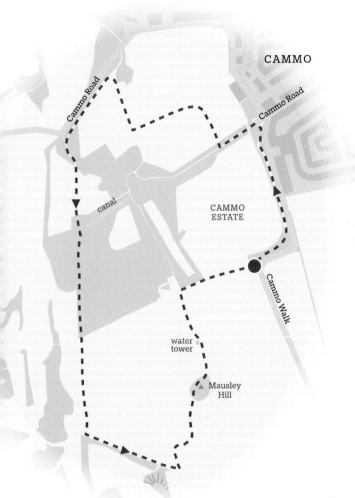

CAMMO

Cammo Road

Cammo Road

canal

CAMMO
ESTATE

Cammo Walk

water
tower

Mausley
Hill

Dalmeny Estate circular

Time 50 minutes
Distance 7.6km/4.7 miles
Terrain forest paths and roads; undulating with one long hill
Lights? no

This is a lovely circular route that follows part of the Queensferry-Cramond Shore Walk, passing a ruined castle and the stately house of Dalmeny Estate.

Whitehouse Bay

● Start on **Hawes Brae** (B924) beneath the Forth Rail Bridge in South Queensferry. The historic 17th-century Hawes Inn is opposite.

SOUTH QUEENSFERRY

B924

▶ Head onto the private road that follows the waterfront. Further on, this goes through a gate and past a cottage called Longcraig Gate and another house on the right.

▶ Keep on the main path, following the Shore Walk (SP Cramond Ferry), with great views over to Leith and Arthur's Seat as you skirt around the tree-fringed Dalmeny Estate.

▶ Eventually this brings you out at the very impressive **Dalmeny House**. Now on tarmac, the route curves round the side of the building where there is a crossroads.

▶ Continue on the main avenue, which is the second on the left: it is on an incline and can be a hard slog.

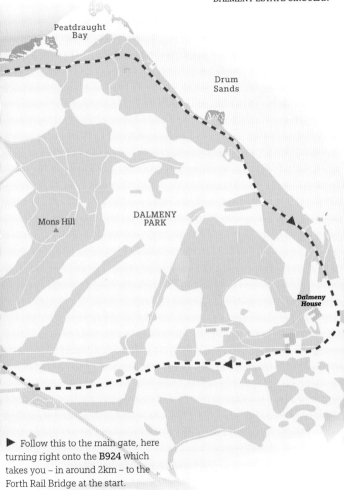

Peatdraught
Bay

Drum
Sands

DALMENY
PARK

Mons Hill

*Dalmeny
House*

▶ Follow this to the main gate, here
turning right onto the **B924** which
takes you – in around 2km – to the
Forth Rail Bridge at the start.

Almondell and Calderwood

Time 25 minutes
Distance 3.8km/2.4 miles
Terrain tarmac, woodland tracks;
mainly flat with two sets of steps
Lights? no

This 220-acre park of two halves has
many enjoyable paths, with
Almondell providing the more
easily navigated riverside and
woodland tracks of this run.

● Start at the **South Car Park** at the
east end of **East Calder**.

▶ Follow the path parallel with the
road to join the main tarmac track.

▶ Continue on this, running
downhill and over **Nasmyth Bridge**
(SP Visitor Centre).

▶ After passing the **visitor centre**
on the right, take the first right,
leaving the tarmac and joining a
woodland path.

▶ Pass the barbecue sites, cross
Mandela Bridge and then run up the
short, steep hill.

▶ At the top of the hill take the steps
to your right to reach a path through
the forest (can be muddy), with fine
views over the fields to the left.

▶ The path leads back to the tarmac
track of your outward route. Turn
right, retracing your steps towards
the bridge for around 100m.

▶ Across the bridge, take the first
left, following National Cycle
Network Route 75. There is a large
grassy area to your right.

▶ Turn left over the small wooden
bridge and up the steps. (You can run
up and walk down these steps
several times for an extra workout.)

▶ At the top of the hill, turn left to
return to the tarmac track. Turn right
and run back to the start.

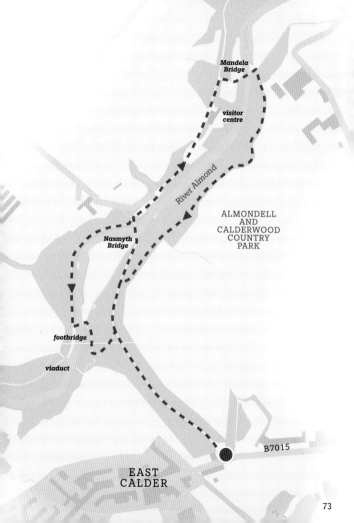

Mandela Bridge

visitor centre

River Almond

ALMONDELL
AND
CALDERWOOD
COUNTRY
PARK

Nasmyth Bridge

footbridge

viaduct

B7015

EAST
CALDER

Beecraigs Country Park

Time 25 minutes
Distance 3.8km/2.4 miles
Terrain woodland paths which can
be muddy at times; one steep hill
and one long incline
Lights? no

Nestled in the Bathgate Hills above
Linlithgow, Beecraigs Country
Park's rugged 913 acres have great
appeal for outdoors lovers of all
types – from high-wire thrill-seekers
to mountain bikers, climbers and
orienteers. This figure-of-eight loop
is full of interest with many
variations to be had.

Children's
Play
Area

Balvormie

🔵 There are several different car
parks at Beecraigs County Park; this
route starts at the **Balvormie** car
park, near the **children's adventure
playground**.

▶ From the car park, follow the red
route (SP **Beecraigs Loch**). This path
is slightly downhill. After around
500m, turn right onto the blue route.

▶ At the top of the hill, turn left
along a narrower path which can be
quite muddy at times. There are also
a few exposed tree roots, so be
careful with your footing.

▶ Where the path splits, keep left to
find yourself doing the red route in
reverse. This brings you out at
Beecraigs Loch.

▶ Follow the track along the shore
of the loch and, at the far end, climb
the flight of steps to continue around
the water.

▶ Turn left, following the lochside,
cross the bridge and turn right and
right again. This will take you up the
hill on the road or the parallel dirt
track towards the **Visitor Centre**.

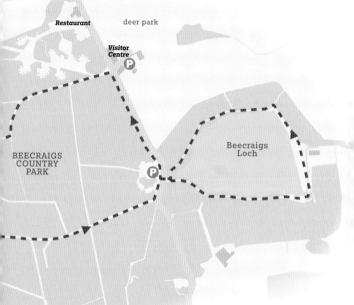

▶ This path brings you out past the children's **adventure playground** on your right to the car park.

◯ Balvormie is also the best access point for a bracing hill run up nearby Cockleroy.

◯ There is a 4km link route from Linlithgow Canal Basin (just above the train station) to Beecraigs, via the canal, a steep roadside bridlepath and Hillhouse Wood.

▶ At the **Visitor Centre**, turn left following signs for **Balvormie**. (For a longer run, keep heading straight up the hill to the top, where you can loop round Hillhouse Wood before rejoining the route.)

Linlithgow Loch

Time 25 minutes
Distance 3.7km/2.3 miles
Terrain dirt tracks and tarmac; flat
Lights? only for short sections

This run makes a circuit of the picturesque Linlithgow Loch, just a couple of minutes from the town's train station. Frequent trains take just 20 minutes from Edinburgh city centre. For a short, regular off-road run, it doesn't get much better than this.

🏃 Start at the car park by **Linlithgow Palace** (charge Mon-Sat 8am-6pm). (Alternatively, there is a free lochside car park behind the health centre – entry off St Ninians Road – but it is often busy.)

▶ Run down the steps towards the water and turn left, following the tarmac path along the busier south shore. You may find swans and geese straddling the path on some sections, but they will pay little heed to you.

▶ At the far end of the loch, cross a small bridge and keep right. This side has a wilder, more tranquil feel and the views of **Linlithgow Palace** from here are hard to beat.

▶ Just beyond the end of the loch, the path meets the road. Turn sharp right to go through a gate (SP **Linlithgow Loch**) instead. This path takes you to another gate and the road further down.

▶ Turn right (SP Town Centre Linlithgow Loch 2.3m circular).

▶ Turn first right after around 100m (SP Linlithgow Loch 2.3m circular Palace and Peel): this tarmac path leads back down towards the loch between the houses and church. Cross a small bridge and follow the path past the swings, heading towards the palace.

▶ Follow the path round the Peel (palace grounds), keeping the water on your right. As you approach the start point, aim for the wall and turn right to return up the steps to the **car park**.

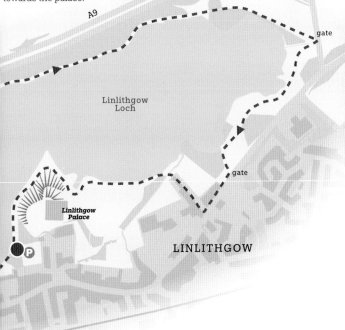

A9

Linlithgow Loch

gate

gate

Linlithgow Palace

LINLITHGOW

WEST LOTHIAN

The Pentland Hills

To the southwest of the capital, the north-facing slopes of the Pentland Hill range dominate the skyline. Its proximity to the city makes this 10,000 hectares of Regional Park well-used for outdoor recreation, and the abundant waymarking and good information centres – at Harlaw, Flotterstone and Boghall Farm – add to its accessibility.

With more than 100km of paths, the route possibilities are almost without limit and it is no surprise that the Pentlands are a favourite objective for running groups of all types, as well as significant hill races.

Novice runners should not be put off by the mention of 'hills'; the beauty of the Pentlands is that there are so many routes around the reservoirs that offer a real perspective into the tranquil nature of the hills with next to no climbing.

Finally, near to the northeast edge of the Pentland range, but far removed in character, nestles the secretive Roslin Glen Country Park which provides a very different runnning experience with which to close this chapter.

FIRTH OF FORTH

Leith

EDINBURGH

Currie

Torduff
Reservoir

Swanston

④

③

⑤

A720

Clubbiedean
Reservoir

Bonaly
Reservoir

⑥

MIDLOTHIAN

Eskbank

alerno

①

Harlaw
Reservoir

Glencorse
Reservoir

⑦

reipmuir
eservoir

②

Roslin

⑧

E PENTLANDS

Loganlee
Reservoir

Penicuik

Leadburn

West Linton

Harlaw and beyond

Time 45 minutes
Distance 7.1km/4.4 miles
Terrain muddy paths and road;
undulating; mainly flat with one hill
Lights? no

This lovely run is mainly flat with
just a few gentle hills giving
spectacular views deeper into the
Pentlands and back over the city.

⬤ Start at Harlaw Car Park near the
Harlaw House Ranger Centre just
outside Balerno.

▶ At the Pentland Hills Regional
Park noticeboard, follow the path to
the left over the small bridge and
towards the road. Turn right, passing
the Harlaw Wildlife Garden on
your right.

▶ Follow the road round to the left
and pass through a gate to reach
Harlaw House Ranger Centre.

▶ Turn right directly after the visitor
centre and **Harlaw Reservoir** will be
on your left. Cross the bridge and
follow the path to the left.

▶ As you come to the cobbles, keep
left and run over the bridge and
through a gap in the wall. Turn left
(SP **Black Springs**) with Harlaw
Reservoir on your left and
Threipmuir Reservoir on your right.

▶ After around 200m, take the
path on your left and continue for
around 1000m to a stile on your right
(SP Black Springs).

▶ Cross this and turn left to pass
between two fields.

▶ Where it splits after around 500m,
take the right fork away from the car
park (SP Glencorse). This brings you
up a long, gradual hill.

▶ Pass through the gate and, at the
next gate, turn left (SP Currie) for a
pleasant downhill stretch with great
views over the Forth.

▶ Go through the next gate, passing
forest on your right: this path is rocky
and uneven, so take care.

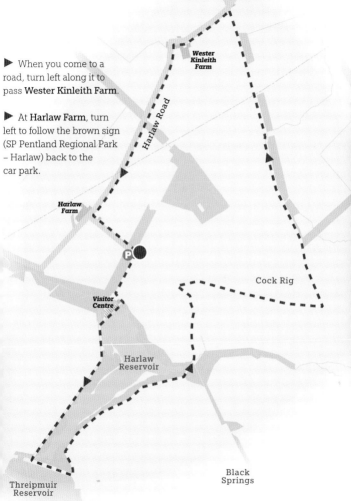

► When you come to a road, turn left along it to pass **Wester Kinleith Farm**.

► At **Harlaw Farm**, turn left to follow the brown sign (SP Pentland Regional Park – Harlaw) back to the car park.

Wester Kinleith Farm

Harlaw Road

Harlaw Farm

Visitor Centre

Cock Rig

Harlaw Reservoir

Threipmuir Reservoir

Black Springs

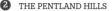

Pentland quartet

Time 1 hour 30 minutes
Distance 14km/8.7 miles
Terrain tarmac and muddy paths;
two steep inclines
Lights? no

This is a beautiful circular route in the hills which takes in four reservoirs. It can be run in either direction, but this route is described anti-clockwise.

🔴 Start at Harlaw Car Park near the **Harlaw House Ranger Centre** just outside Balerno.

▶ At the park noticeboard, follow the path to the left over the bridge and towards the road. Turn right, passing the Harlaw Wildlife Garden on your right.

▶ Follow the road round to the left and pass through a gate to reach Harlaw House Ranger Centre.

▶ Turn right directly after the visitor centre and **Harlaw Reservoir** will be on your left. Cross the bridge and follow the path left.

82

▶ At the end of Harlaw Reservoir, where the path splits, take the right-hand branch to skirt along the edge of **Threipmuir Reservoir**. Keep left and follow the path uphill.

▶ Just after going through a gate, leave the main path for a smaller path to the left (SP Nine Mile Burn 4m, Glencorse 5m).

Visitor Centre

Har
Reser

*Threipmuir
Reservoir*

*Redford
Bridge*

*Bavelaw
Castle*

Green

▶ On meeting the road at the end of this path, turn left (SP Bavelaw) – this is a steep hill!

▶ At the top, follow the road round to the left (SP Penicuik and Glencorse).

▶ As the road continues round to the left, take the dirt path straight ahead and through the gate at the end (SP Penicuk and Glencorse).

▶ You will eventually cross a small bridge and see a house straight ahead. Turn left along the road to pass **Loganlea Reservoir** and reach **Glencorse Reservior**.

▶ Look out for a path on the left about 10m after **Kirkton Farm**; leave the road and head through the gate to climb uphill (SP Colinton by Bonaly, Balerno by Harlaw) – this is a fairly tough section of ascent.

▶ The path soon forks; keep left (SP Balerno by Harlaw). Continue to the gate at the top of the hill and climb the stone steps. From now on, it is all flat or downhill.

▶ After passing through another gate, turn right to return to the start.

Torduff and Bonaly

Time 25 minutes
Distance 3.4km/2.1 miles
Terrain tarmac, grassy and stony paths; two steep hills
Lights? no

This is a great short, hard run in the Pentland Hills where you feel miles away from the city.

⬤ Start on **Bonaly Road**, just after the bridge over the city bypass (**A720**).

▶ Turning right along **Torduff Road**, pass the water treatment works on an uphill to **Torduff Reservoir**.

▶ Go through the gate at the bottom of the reservoir, continuing along the road with the water on your left.

▶ As the road loops round the top of the reservoir at the southern end, cross the bridge and carry straight on through the gate, leaving the road behind (SP Bonaly and Dreghorn).

▶ This grassy path leads you through two further gates and aims for a forest. Go through the gate at the start of the forest and turn right.

▶ Continue along this path until you reach a wider path perpendicular to it. Turn left down the hill (SP **Bonaly**).

▶ Go through the gate at the bottom, passing the car park and **Scout Camp**. Follow the road back round to the start.

Torduff
Golf
Course

Tordu
Reserv

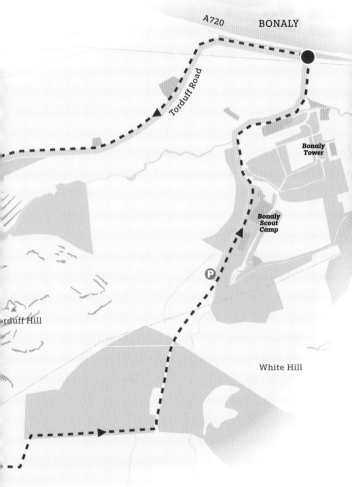

BONALY

A720

Torduff Road

Bonaly
Tower

Bonaly
Scout
Camp

rduff Hill

White Hill

Bonaly and Blinkbonny

Time 1 hour
Distance 9.7km/6 miles
Terrain roads, dirt tracks and
cyclepath; some moderate inclines,
with two steep hills
Lights? no

Sure to be a favourite for many users
of this guide, this hour-long circuit
offers a swift retreat from the city for
fresh air and beautiful hill views.

CURRIE

BLINKBONNY

Currie
Baptist
Church

Kinleith Burn

Kirkgate

Easter
Kinleith

🔘 Start on **Bonaly Road**, just after the
bridge over the city bypass (A720).

▶ Turning right along Torduff Road,
pass the water treatment works on an
uphill to **Torduff Reservoir**.

▶ Go through the gate at the bottom
of the reservoir, continuing along the
road with the reservoir on your left.

▶ As the road loops round the top of
the reservoir at the southern end, cross
two bridges, heading up the incline
towards **Clubbiedean Reservoir**. This
is the last incline till near the end of
the route.

▶ The road meanders round the
base of the Pentlands towards Middle
and Easter Kinleith Farms, with

spectacular views.

▶ Approaching **Easter Kinleith
Farm**, the road veers sharply left
(SP Harlaw). Keep on the road.

▶ At a T-junction, turn right down

JUNIPER GREEN

West Mill Rd.

Water of Leith

BONALY

A720 Edinburgh By-Pass

Bonaly Road

Torduff Reservoir

Warklaw Hill

Clubbiedean Reservoir

path which you take to the right.

► Next turn right onto the **Water of Leith** Walkway and head eastwards towards the city centre for around 3km, following the brown signs.

the hill on **Kirkgate**.

► Towards the bottom, after the cemetery on your right, turn left onto a dirt track just before some cottages at the small **Currie Baptist Church**.

► Where you see a car park with a derelict engine shed, look for the

► Pass under the city bypass and continue along the water until you reach a minor road, where you turn right, then left up to **West Mill Road**. This is a very steep hill, but worth the effort as you are nearly finished.

► Cross the junction to **Bonaly Road** (another hill!) and follow the road past Bonaly Primary School, over the bypass and back to

Hillend and Swanston

Time 25 minutes
Distance 3.5km/2.2 miles
Terrain steep hill at the start of the route, good paths but can be rocky underfoot
Lights? no

This route on the northern slopes of the Pentlands starts with a steep hill, but the views over Edinburgh and across the Forth from the top make it all worthwhile.

🔵 Start at the car park just off the A702 at the bottom of the road to the **Midlothian Snow Sports Centre** (the longest dry ski slope in Europe!).

▶ Follow the path to the left of the road which then crosses over to the right side and you begin the steep incline. This bit can be walked as a good warm up if you don't fancy running it!

▶ The golf course is on your right and the ski centre on your left – if you need a breather make sure you turn round to admire the views!

▶ Pass through the gate and follow the path traversing the hill, following the fence.

▶ Once you reach the sign, follow the path to the right (SP Capital View Walk/Swanston).

▶ Follow the path downhill (there is a nice bit in the middle of this path that can be used for some interval hill runs) and pass through the gate.

▶ Keep left when the path splits, entering the gate and passing through the picturesque village of **Swanston** with thatched cottages.

▶ Turn right at the sign (SP Lothianburn/Capital View Walk). Pass the steadings on the right and you will be running parallel with the bypass.

▶ This path takes you out at the A702 – turn right and run along the pavement, turning right after the Steading Bar to return to the car park.

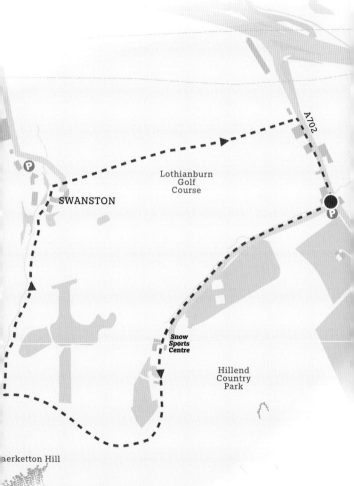

A702

P

SWANSTON

Lothianburn
Golf
Course

Snow
Sports
Centre

Hillend
Country
Park

aerketton Hill

Caerketton Hill from Boghall

Time 40 minutes

Distance 4.8km/3 miles

Terrain paths and tracks, rocky in parts with steep inclines

Lights? no

Save this high-level run for a sunny day; the view from the top is fantastic. The route up is fairly steep, so if you are struggling don't be afraid to walk, you are still getting exercise!

● Start at **Boghall Farm**, the headquarters of The Pentlands Regional Park.

▶ Pass through two gates (SP Boghall Glen, Hillend & Swanston).

▶ Follow fenced path uphill.

▶ Just after the cottage, go through the gate on the left (SP Pentland Path).

▶ Join the main path and follow it as it climbs steadily, passing through several gates or stiles.

▶ Continue on the path as it curves right round the hill, which will take you out to **Windy Door Nick**.

Allermt Hill

▶ Turn right here and follow the fence to the summit of **Caerketton Hill**.

▶ Follow the path as it descends the hill, which is fairly steep, and at the bottom turn right following the sign for Boghall.

▶ At the next signpost turn right again for Boghall. Follow the contour of the hill by the wood till you come to open land.

▶ Turn left downhill and back to the start.

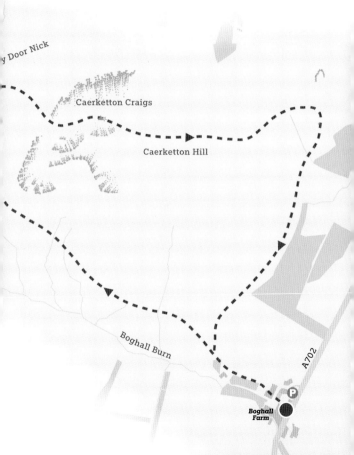

Door Nick

Caerketton Craigs

Caerketton Hill

Boghall Burn

A702

Boghall
Farm

Flotterstone flyer

Time 30 minutes
Distance 4.5km/2.8 miles
Terrain road and muddy
paths; one steep hill
Lights? no

This quick, scenic
route starts by the
popular Flotterstone
Inn on the southeast
side of the Pentlands.
It's a good introduction to
running off-road.

Start at **Flotterstone Car Park** just
off the **A702** Biggar road.

▶ Head along the road (SP
Glencorse Reservior 1m) until you
meet a path on the right after around
1km (SP Castle Law).

▶ Leave the road here and pass
through the gate to climb a fairly
steep hill.

▶ As it levels out, you will see a
building straight ahead. Go left
(SP **Glencorse Reservoir**). There is
an infrequently used **military firing
range** on your right.

▶ Continue traversing the slopes, then follow the signpost left downhill alongside trees to **Glencorse Reservoir**.

▶ As you come to the bottom of the path and hit the road, turn left.

▶ At the end of the reservoir you will pass **Glen Cottage**. Shortly after, drop downhill to the right (SP Flotterstone by **Old Filter Beds**), then follow the path round to the left.

▶ This will bring you out at the road you started on. Turn right and head back to the car park.

DANGER:
CASTLELAW
FIRING
RANGES

Flotterstone Inn

Roslin Glen quest

Time 1 hour
Distance 7km/4.4 miles
Terrain narrow woodland trails, public roads and cyclepaths; hilly
Lights? only in Loanhead

Roslin, situated only 11km from Edinburgh city centre, is home to historic Rosslyn Chapel. This hilly route is strenuous with narrow, muddy and rutted riverside trails.

● Start from the car park at **Rosslyn Chapel**. Head back towards Roslin and turn right onto **Manse Road**.

▶ Carry on along the single-track road until it forks just past the farms and houses. Follow the cyclepath to the right and continue until it ends at Station Road in **Loanhead**.

▶ Follow Station Road and turn left onto High Street, then first right along Church Street.

▶ At the police station, follow the road round to the left (**Polton Road**). Follow this downhill, taking care as this is a narrow road and traffic can be fast.

▶ At the bottom, you will see a small gate on the right (SP Roslin 5km) – if you have crossed a bridge, you have gone too far.

▶ Take this narrow path uphill and enter a gate on the left at the top (SP Roslin via Riverside Path).

ROSLIN

Manse Roa

● **Rosslyn Chapel**

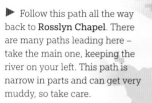

LOANHEAD

Polton Road

► Follow this path all the way back to **Rosslyn Chapel**. There are many paths leading here – take the main one, keeping the river on your left. This path is narrow in parts and can get very muddy, so take care.

Bilston Burn

Bilston Wood

POLTON

The Maiden Castle

Research Centre

River North Esk

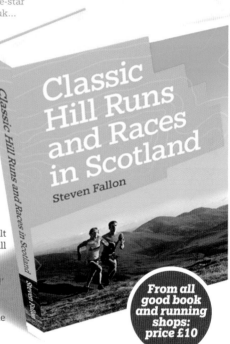